IT'S YOUR BIRTHDAY,

YOU CAN LAUGH

IF YOU WANT TO.

☞ **W9-BKA-234**

DESIGN: MARK EIMER; ILLUSTRATION: KIM EBNER

WRITTEN BY:

Chris Brethwaite, Bill Bridgeman,

Jennifer Fujita, Bill Gray,

Marn Jensen, Allyson Jones,

Kevin Kinzer, Mark Oatman,

Dee Ann Stewart, Dan Taylor

and Myra Zirkle.

Birthdays are like money...

the more you have, the more

people assume you know

what you're doing.

Even if you could buy youth,

your charge cards would

probably all be too close

to the limit.

Don't smirk when you make

your birthday wish, or everyone will

know what you wished for.

Let your laughter be the loudest noisemaker at your party.

Don't celebrate your birthday
by looking at old pictures
of yourself. In fact, avoid that
on other days, too.

A friend in need is probably

a middle-aged friend.

It's impolite to "accidentally"

spill your soup on the waiters

gathered around your table

to sing "Happy Birthday."

Just one piece of cake

is plenty if you cut it

big enough.

After a certain age,

any limbo contest

could be your last.

You're not old until you start

tipping maitre d's to seat you

by the rest room.

After the party, it's good luck

to eat all the remaining

birthday cake yourself.

To do something you love

is to drink from the

Fountain of Youth.

Never forget that there is such a thing as too many knicknacks.

You'll be a lot happier

with growing older when you

stop expecting music to be as

good as it used to be.

If birthdays were only for

the young, the cake would be

a lot tougher.

19

Most of the cultures

that revere old age have

died out by now.

Take time to stop and pretend

you can still smell the roses.

It's OK if you see your childhood lunch box in an antique store.

22

**Frame a picture of yourself
from junior high and marvel
at your improvements.**

It could be worse.

Light from birthday candles

could be fluorescent.

The inability to sense

a fallen bra strap is the

first sign of old age.

We all get older,

but it takes some of us

a lot longer to get old.

The bigger the piece of

birthday cake, the more

ice cream you get to take

to balance the plate.

Curse the alarm clock,

but celebrate the morning.

Knowing the weather is one thing. Knowing the barometric pressure in the mid-Atlantic states is quite another.

No matter how young you feel, don't pierce anything you haven't already pierced.

If you see anyone under 16

wearing what you're wearing,

change what you're wearing.

The earlier in the day you

have to stop drinking coffee,

the older you are.

Bad news:

The aging process has begun.

Good news:

There's no paperwork.

You actually can teach an old dog new tricks. He just can't remember them for very long.

After three hours,

it's no longer called

"resting your eyes."

Suddenly, your back is more

important than your front.

If you keep staring at

those lines around your eyes

in the rearview mirror,

you'll miss your exit.

You can't really burn off
extra calories by eating
your birthday cake with
a heavy fork.

The best present is the one

you incessantly hinted for.

If you don't blow out all

the candles, that's OK.

They look better lit.

It's not necessary to

specify your age in order to

have a fun birthday.

Before you thank someone for their hilarious "gag" gift, make sure it was intended as a hilarious "gag" gift.

No matter what flavor birthday cake is served, no matter what flavor ice cream accompanies it, chocolate sauce is appropriate, and to be encouraged.

What are old women

with really long hair

trying to prove?

Don't fight growing older.

You'll probably need all the

energy you've got left

for staircases.

When all of your outfits seem

to make your butt look big,

perhaps it's not the outfits

that are doing it.

You'll never regret saving

the last piece of birthday cake

for breakfast.

The squeaky joint

gets the ointment.

The harder you try

to enjoy your birthday,

the less you will.

Once you've tried on all the swimsuits, have some ice cream.

When you start having trouble

bending over, it's time to

stop dropping things.

If you're going over the hill anyway, take a kite.

Getting older is no excuse

for letting polyester sneak into

your wardrobe.

If you've ever even thought about putting a lawn chair in your driveway, you are old.

Wear a smile for another year

and the year will smile back.

Aging is nature's way of saying,

"You can't have too big

a medicine chest."

You're only as old as you feel.

Just don't go by how you feel

first thing in the morning.

Nobody seems to notice

if you look your age when

you're smiling.

Be sure to get all your

birthday pictures taken

while only the candles are

lighting the room.

You're not old until you don't give back the baseballs that land in your yard.

The more candles on your cake,

the more icing minisnacks

you'll have after everyone

goes home.

You know you're getting older

when your high school reunion

consists of everyone walking

out of a magic corn field.

Old age is defined not by

calendars, but by attitudes.

Keep buying cereal for the prize, not the bran content.

Before blowing out candles,

ensure against embarrassment

by hiring kids to join in the fun.

Half the fun of your birthday

party is watching your friends

have so much fun.

Sometimes when you stop

and take a good hard look at

yourself, you realize you're

spending too much time

looking at yourself.

Look on the bright side:

You could be excited about

finding hairs that aren't gray.

You can still shake a leg.

And, coincidentally, that will

now be your idea of a fun time.

Eliminate the phrase "teensy slice of cake" from your vocabulary for the day.

Pin-the-Tail-on-the-Donkey

goes a little faster when all the

players can forego the blindfold

and just take off their

glasses instead.

Any sport that you play

that doesn't make you sore

the next day probably isn't

actually considered a sport.

Think of each birthday as a gift.

A gift when you get other gifts.

If you can, try to think of squeaky knees, ankles and knuckles as your body applauding you for making it through another year.

If you can tell what color your plate is, you don't have enough cake and ice cream.

The friends who sing "Happy Birthday" to you probably aren't trying to be sarcastic.

The best thing about birthdays

is when the personal mail

outweighs the bills.

If birthdays make you

a little sad, it's probably

because you're human.

You've taken your daily "multiple vitamins plus iron and zinc," now eat whatever the heck you want.

The inventor of the camcorder

obviously never had to hold his

stomach in for a picture.

Like an airplane landing, any birthday you can walk away from is a good birthday.

If you begin talking

to yourself, try to keep it

upbeat and cheery.

Call in sick on your friends'

birthdays, too.

Look in the paper and find a star who shares your birthday and is older than you.

Cutting back on fried foods just means you won't have to soak your pans as long before you put them in the dishwasher.

Birthday wishes are more

likely to come true when

children help you

blow out the candles.

Time for the best birthday

party game of all:

Let's pretend we're young!

The video camera will add

10 pounds anyway, so eat

as much cake as you want.

No matter how much it seems like it, the people who publish lingerie catalogues aren't doing it just to taunt you.

From now on, your only short

skirt is on a bathing suit.

The best thing about having

the big party at your house

is that no matter how many

people there are, you always

get the recliner.

Having your home movies colorized is a pretty expensive way to feel younger.

Once most of your hair

has fallen out, you can

stop coloring it.

Wearing a party hat is more important than preserving a hairstyle.

Display your birthday cards proudly. You've earned and deserve each one.